The Magical Works of
Heinrich-Cornelius Agrippa

Copyright © 2024

Éditions Unicursal Publishers

unicursal.ca

ISBN 978-2-89806-609-2 (Paperback)
ISBN 978-2-89806-610-8 (Hardcover)

First English Edition, Ostara 2024

THE
MAGICAL
WORKS
OF
HEINRICH-CORNELIUS
AGRIPPA,

BY PETER DE ABANO,

With Occult Secrets.

AT LIEGE

LES ŒUVRES MAGIQUES DE HENRI - CORNEILLE AGRIPPA,

Par PIERRE D'ABAN,

Avec des Secrets occultes.

A LIEGE

PETER DE ABANO

HEPTAMERON

OR

MAGICAL ELEMENTS

of PETER DE ABANO,
Philosopher.

In the former book, which is the fourth book of *Agrippa*, it is sufficiently spoken concerning Magical Ceremonies, and Initiations. But because he seemeth to have written to the learned, and well-experienced in this art; because he doth not specially treat of the Ceremonies, but rather speaketh of them in general, it was therefore thought good to adde hereunto the Magical Elements of *Peter de Abano*: that those who are hitherto ignorant, and have not tasted of Magical Superstitions, may have them in readiness, how they may exercise themselves therein, for we see in this book, as it were a certain introduction of Magical vanity; and, as if they were in present exercise, they may behold the distinct functions of spirits, how they may be drawn to discourse and communication; what is to be done every day, and every hour; and how they shall be read, as if they were described sillable by sillable.

In brief, in this book are kept the principles of Magical conveyances. But because the greatest power is attributed to the Circles, for they are certain fortresses to defend the operators safe from the evil Spirits. In the first place we will treat concerning the composition of a Circle.

Of the Circle, & the Composition thereof.

The form of Circles is not alwaies one and the same; but useth to be changed, according to the order of the Spirits that are to be called, their places, times, dayes and hours. For in making a Circle, it ought to be considered in what time of the year, what day, and what hour, that you make the Circle; what Spirits you would call, to what Star and Region they do belong, and what functions they have.

Therefore let there be made three Circles of the latitude of nine foot, and let them be distant one from another a hands breadth; and in the middle Circle, first, write: 1° The name of the hour wherein you do the work; 2° Write the name of the Angel of the hour; 3° The Sigil of the Angel of the hour; 4° The name of the Angel that ruleth that day wherein you do the work, and the names of his ministers; 5° The name of the present time; 6° The name of the Spirits ruling in that part of time, and their Presidents; 7° The name of the head of the Signe ruling in that part of time wherein you work; 8° The name of the earth, according to that part of time wherein you work; 9° And for the compleating of the middle Circle, Write the name of the Sun and of the Moon, according to the said rule of time; for as the time is changed, so the names are to be altered. And in the outermost Circle, let there be drawn in the four Angles, the names of the presidential Angels of the Air, that day wherein you would do this work; to wit, the name of the King and his three Ministers. Without the Circle, in four Angles, let *Pentagones* be made. In the inner Circle let there be written four divine names with crosses interposed in the middle of the Circle; to wit, towards the East let there be written *Alpha*, and towards the West let there be written *Omega*; and let a cross divide the middle of the Circle. When the Circle is thus finished, according to the rule now before written, you shall proceed.

Of the Names of the Hours, & the Angels ruling them.

It is also to be known, that the Angels do rule the hours in a successive order, according to the course of the heavens, and Planets unto which they are subject; so that that Spirit which governeth the day, ruleth also the first hour of the day; the second from this governeth the second hour; the third; the third hour, and so consequently. And when seven Planets and hours have made their revolution, it returneth again to the first which ruleth the day. Therefore we shall first speak of the names of the hours:

Hours of the Day.	Hours of the Night.
1. Yayn.	13. Beron.
2. Janor.	14. Barol.
3. Nasnia.	15. Thami.
4. Salla.	16. Athir.
5. Sadedali.	17. Mathon.
6. Thamur.	18. Rana.
7. Ourer.	19. Netos.
8. Thamie.	20. Tafrac.
9. Neron.	21. Sassur.
10. Jayon.	22. Agla.
11. Abai.	23. Calerva.
12. Natalon.	24. Salam.

Of the names of the Angels and their Sigils, it shall be spoken in their proper places. Now let us take a view of the names of the times. A year therefore is fourfold, and is divided into the Spring, Summer, Harvest and Winter; the names whereof are these:

The Spring . . . . Talvi;
The Summer . . . . Gasmaran;
Autumne. . . . . Ardarael;
Winter. . . . . Fallas.

The Angels of the Spring.
Caracasa, Core, Amatiel, Commissoros.

Head of the signe: Spugliguel.
Name of the Earth: Amadai.
Name of the Sun: Abraym.
Name of the Moon: Agusita.

The Angels of the Summer.
Gargatel, Tariel, Gaviel.

Head of the signe:	Tubiel.
Name of the Earth:	Festativi.
Name of the Sun:	Athemay.
Name of the Moon:	Armatas.

The Angels of Autumne.
Tarquam, Guabarel.

Head of the signe:	Tarquaret.
Name of the Earth:	Rabianara.
Name of the Sun:	Abragini.
Name of the Moon:	Matasignais.

The Angels of Winter.
Amabael, Ctarari.

Head of the signe:	Altarib.
Name of the Earth:	Gerenia.
Name of the Sun:	Commutaf.
Name of the Moon:	Affaterim.

THE CONSECRATIONS & BENEDICTIONS.

Of the Benediction of the Circle.

When the Circle is ritely perfected, sprinkle the same with holy or purging water, and say:

Asperges me, Domine, hyssopo & mundabor: lavabia, & super nivem dealbabor.

The Benediction of Perfumes.

The perfumes which will be used for fumigations, say the following blessing, extending your hand over the perfumes:

God of Abraham, God of Isaac, God of Jacob, bless here the creatures of these kindes, that they may fill up the power and vertue of their odours; so that neither the enemy, nor any false imagination, may be able to enter into them: per Dominum nostrum Jesum-Christum, &c.

Then let them be sprinkled with holy water.

The Exorcisme of the fire upon which the Perfumes are to be put.

The fire which is to be used for suffumigations, is to be in a new vessel of earth or iron; and let it be exorcised after this manner, extending the hand:

I exorcise thee, O thou creature of fire, by him by whom all things are made, that forthwith thou cast away every phantasme from thee, that it shall not be able to do any hurt in anything.

Then say:

Bless, O Lord, this creature of fire, and sanctfie it, that it may be blessed to set forth the praise of thy holy name, that no hurt may come to the Exorcisers or Spectators: through our Lord Jesus Christ, &c.

Of the Garment & Pentacle.

Let it be a Priests Garment, if it can be had, let it be of linen, and clean.

Then take this Pentacle made in the day and hour of *Mercury*, the Moon increasing, written in parchment made of a Kids skin. But first let there be said over it the Mass of the holy Ghost, and let it be sprinkled with water of baptism.

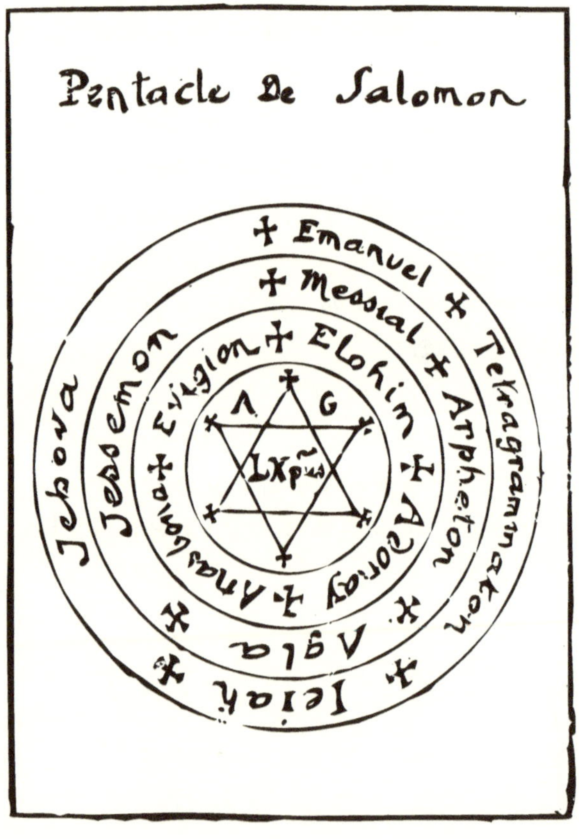

Oration to be said, when the Vesture is put on.

*A*ncor, *Amacor, Amides, Theodonias, Anitor; by the merits of thy Angel, O Lord, I will put on the Garments of Salvation, that this which I desire I may bring to effect: through thee the most holy Adonay, whose kingdom endureth for ever and ever. Amen.*

Of the manner of working.

Let the Moon be increasing and equal, if it may then be done, and let her not be com bust. The Operator ought to be clean and purified by the space of nine dayes before the beginning of the work, and to be confessed, and receive the holy Communion. Let him have ready the perfume appropriated to the day wherein he would perform the work. He ought also to have holy water from a Priest, and a new earthen vessel with fire, a Vesture and a Pentacle; and let all these things be rightly and duly consecrated and prepared.

Let one of the servants carry the earthen vessel full of fire, and the perfumes, and let another bear the Book, another the Garment and Pentacle, and let the master carry the Sword over which there must be said one mass of the Holy Ghost; and on the middle of the Sword, let there be written this name, *Agla* ✠, and on the other side thereof, this name ✠ *On* ✠. And as he goeth to the consecrated place, let him continually read Letanies, the servants answering. And when he cometh to the place where he will erect the Circle, let him draw the lines of the Circle, as we have before taught: and after he hath made it, let him sprinkle the Circle with holy water, saying:

Asperges me, Domine, hyssopo & mundabor: lavabis me, & super nivem dealbabor.

The Master therefore ought to be purified with fasting, chastity, and abstinency from all luxury the space of seven whole dayes before the day of the operation. And on the day that he would do the work, being clothed with pure garments, and furnished with Pentacles, Perfumes, and other things necessary hereunto, let him enter the Circle, and call the Angels from the four parts of the World, which do govern the seven Planets the seven dayes of the week, Colours and Metals; whose name you shall see in their places. And with bended knees invocating the said Angels particularly, let him say:

O Angels, be favourable to me and help me in my affairs and in my requests.

Then let him call the Angels from the four parts of the World, that rule the Air the same day wherein he doth the work or experiment. And having implored specially all the Names and Spirits written in the Circle, let him say:

O all of you, I conjure you and call you to witness by the siege of Adonay, by Aghios, O Theos, Ischyros, Athanatos, Paracletus, Alpha & Omega, and by these three Secret Names: Agla, On, Tetragrammaton, that you must accomplish today what I ask.

These things being performed, let him read the Conjuration assigned for the day wherein he maketh the experiments, as we have before spoken; but if they shall be obstinate and refractory, and will not yield themselves obedient, neither to the Conjuration assigned to the day, nor to the prayers before made, then use the Conjurations and Exorcismes following.

Exorcisme of the Spirits of the Air.

We, made in the image of God, endowed with the power of God, and made by His will, we exorcise you (here he will name the spirits he wishes, of whatever orders they may be) by the Almighty, most established, strong and admirable name of God, EL, and command you by Him who said, and all was done; and by all the names of God: Adonay, El, Elohim, Zebaoth, Elion, Escerchie, Iah, Tetragrammaton, Saday, the Lord God, Most High: we exorcise you and forcefully command you to appear at once around this Circle, in a beautiful form, that is, human, and without any deformity or blemish. Come all thus, because we command you, by the name Y and V, which Adam heard and spoke; and by the name of God, Agla, which Lot heard and which made him and his family safe, and by the name Iod which Jacob heard from the Angel with whom he wrestled and by which he was delivered from the hand of his brother Esau; and by the name Anephexeton, which Aaron heard, and which made him speak and wise; and by the name Zebaoth, which Moses uttered, and turned all the rivers and marshes of Egypt into blood; and by the name Escerchie Oriston, which Moses named, and brought out of the rivers the frogs that invaded the houses of the Egyptians; and by the name Elion, which Moses pronounced, and caused such a great hail to fall that no such hail has been seen since the beginning of the world; and by the name Adonay, which Moses named, and produced that prodigious quantity of locusts that appeared in Egypt and ate what had not been destroyed by the hail; and by the name Schemes Amathia, which Joshua named, and stopped the course of the Sun, and by the name Alpha and Omega, which Daniel named, by which he destroyed Bel and killed the Dragon; and by the name Emmanuel, which the three children: Sidrach, Misach and Abdenago sang in the fiery furnace, and by which they were delivered; and by *Aghios*, and by the Seat of *Adonay*, and by *O Theos Ischiros, Athanatos, Paracletus*; and by these three Secret Names: *Agla, On, Tetragrammaton*, I conjure you and take you to witness, and by all these names, and by all the names of our Lord, God almighty, true and living; you who by your sin have been cast out of Heaven and cast into Hell, we strongly exorcise and command you by Him who having said, and all was done, to whom all creatures obey; and by this terrible judgment of God which is to be feared; and by the sea which is an element on which no one can count anything certain, transparent as glass, which is in the presence of the divine Majesty, ready to ascend according to the power God will give it; and by the four divine animals T. which are on the degrees of the seat of the divine Majesty, and which have eyes before and behind; and by the Fire which surrounds his Throne; and because which is called the Church of God; and by the supreme wisdom of *Almighty God*; we strongly exorcise you to appear before this Circle, to do our will in whatever we please, by the seat of *Balmachia* and by that name *Primeumaton*, which Moses named and precipitated *Datan, Corel* and

Abiron into the depths of the abysses; and by virtue of that same name Primeumaton, which makes all the heavenly, earthly Militia, and the Underworld tremble; we curse you, we deprive you of all offices and functions, and of all pleasures you may have, we place and relegate you to eternal fire and to the lake of fire and brimstone; into the depths of the Abyss, and until the last day of judgment, if you do not appear to us at once, before this Circle, to do our will in all things; come by these names Adonay, Zebaoth, Adonay, come, come, Adonay commands you, this most powerful and most to be feared King of kings, whose strength and power no creature can evade. If you persist in your extreme obstinacy, and if before this Circle you do not appear to us at once, gentle and affable, you can expect only a lamentable and miserable ruin, and a fire that can never be extinguished. Come then in the name of Adonay Zebaoth, Adonay, Amioram. Come, come, why do you delay? Hurry at once! This is commanded you by Adonay Saday, the King of kings, El Aty, Titeip, Azia, Hyn, Jen, Minosel, Achadan, Uay, Vaa, Ey, Haa, Eye, Exe, à El, El, El, à Hy, Hau, Hau, Hau, Va, Va, Va, Va.

Teachings will be found in the Grimoire of Pope Honorius, Rome edition, 1670.

Orison to God, to be said in the four parts of the World, in the Circle.

Amorule, Tancha, Latisten, Rabur, Escha, Aladia, Alpha & Omega, Leyste, Oriston, Adonay: O my most merciful heavenly Father, have mercy upon me, although a sinner; make appear the arm of thy power in me this day (although thy unworthy child) against these obstinate and pernicious Spirits, that I by thy will may be made a contemplator of thy divine works, and may be illustrated with all wisdom, and alwaies worship and glorifie thy name. I humbly implore and beseech thee, that these Spirits which I call by thy judgement, may be bound and constrained to come, and give true and perfect answers to those things which I shall ask them, and that they may declare and shew unto us those things which by me or us shall be commanded them, not hurting any creature, neither injuring nor terrifying me or my fellows, nor hurting any other creature, and affrighting no man; but let them be obedient to my requests, in all these things which I command them.

Then let him stand in the middle of the Circle, and hold his hand towards the Pentacle, and say:

I call you by the virtue of the Pentacle of Solomon; give me a true answer.

Let him wait a moment, then say:

Seat of Beretaneuse, Baldachia, Paumachia and Apologia, I invoke you by the Kings, and the magnanimous Powers, and the very powerful Princes, by the spirit of Liachidae, minister of Tartarus; Primac, who are here the Prince of the Seat of Apologia in the ninth cohort, I conjure you, and equipped with the virtue of the Supreme Majesty, I command you powerfully by Him who having said, and all was done, and to whom all creatures obey, and by this ineffable name, Tetragrammaton, Jehovah, who is the source and origin of all centuries, in whose name the ele-ments merge, the air is struck and shaken, the sea goes against its common course, the fire goes out, the earth trembles, all the celestial, terrestrial and infernal armies tremble, are disturbed and are in a violent movement of ruin, this is why at the moment and without any pretext of delay for any occasion whatever, come from all parts of the World, and answer me properly on everything I ask you. Come now and without any delay, as we wish, conjured as you are by the name of God Helioren, eternal, living and true; and do what we command you, always persisting in our intentions until the end; appear before us, visible, gentle and affable, answering us with a clear and intelligible voice, and without any ambiguity.

Visions & Apparitions.

These things being done exactly, there will appear an infinity of visions and phantoms playing all kinds of musical instruments; the Spirits do this to frighten the Disciples and force them to leave the Circle, because they can do nothing against the one who carries out the operation; then you will see an infinity of people armed with arrows, with a multitude of horrible beasts standing ready to devour the Disciples who, however, have nothing to fear. Then, the Priest or Exorcist, extending his hand over the Pentacle, must say:

May your prestige cease by the virtue of the crucified God.

Then, the Spirits will be forced to obey the Exorcist, and the Disciples will be at peace and will no longer see horrible forms. Then let the Exorcist say, stretching out his hand to the Pentacle:

Behold the Pentacle of Solomon that I present to you. Here is also the person of the Master in the middle of the exorcism, who is very well equipped by the power of God, fearless and provided with everything, who being very powerful in strength, has invoked you by exorcising you, and calls you. Come then, and haste, by virtue of these names: Age, Saraye, Aye, Saraye, do not delay coming by the eternal names of the living and true God, Eloy, Circhina, Rabur; and by this Pentacle which powerfully commands over you, and by the virtue of the celestial Spirits, your Masters, and by the person of the Exorcist, conjured as you are, haste, and obey your Master who is called Octinomos.

This being done, blow into the four corners of the world, and you will immediately see great movements. Then say:

Why are you delaying? What are you doing? Prepare to obey your Master promptly, in the name of Lord Bathat or Vachat rushing towards Abrac, occurring Abeor on Aberer.

Then they will come immediately in their own forms, and when you see them near the Circle, show them the Pentacle covered with a Holy Shroud, uncover it for then, and say:

This is your last term; do not be disobedient.

Immediately, you will see them in a peaceful form, and they will say:

Ask what you want, we are ready to obey your commandments, because the Lord has submitted to us.

And when they have appeared thus, say to them:

Welcome, most noble Spirits or Kings, because I have called you by Him in whose name every knee must bent, of the celestial, terrestrial and infernal; in whose hand are the kingdoms of all kings, and to whose majesty no one can be contrary; this is why I force you to remain before this Circle, visible and affable, without you being able to leave before my saying, and until you have accomplished my will, exactly and without any deception, by the virtue and power of Him who gave to the sea limits which it cannot pass and which it cannot overflow by the law of this power, namely the Most High God, King, Lord, who created all things. Amen.

Then command what you will, and it shall be done. Afterwards license them thus:

In the name of the Father ✠ and of the Son ✠ and of the Holy Spirit ✠: go in peace to your abodes, and may peace be between you and us; and always be ready to come when you will be called.

These are the things which *Peter de Abano* hath spoken concerning Magical Elements.

But that you may the better know the manner of composing a Circle, I will set down one Scheme; so that if any one would make a Circle in Spring-time for the first hour of Lords day, it must be in the same manner as is the figure following. It remaineth now, that we explain the week, the several dayes thereof : and first of the Lords day.

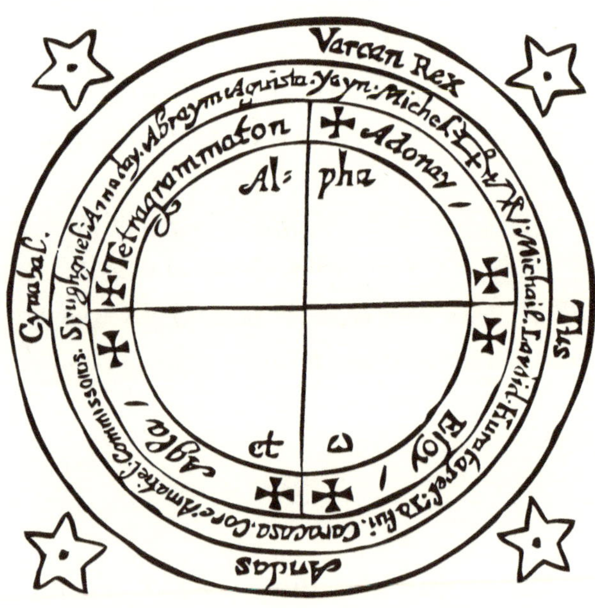

The figure of a Circle for the first hour
of the Lords day, in Spring-time.

Considerations of the Lords day.

The Angel of the Lords day, his Sigil, Planet, the Signe of the Planet, and the name of the Fourth Heaven:

The Angels of the Lords day.
Michael, Dardiel, Huratapel.

The Angels of the Air ruling on the Lords day.
Varcan, King.

His Ministers: Tus, Andras, Cynabal.

*The winde under which are the said Angels
of the Air.*
Boreas (The North-winde.)

*The Angel of the Fourth Heaven, ruling on the
Lords day, which ought to be called from the four
parts of the World.*

At the East.
Samael, Gabriel, Baciel,
Vionatrabar, Atel.

At the West.
Anael, Burchat, Pabel,
Suceratos, Vestael, Capabili.

At the North.
Aiel, Sapiel, Aniel *or* Aquiel,
Matuyel, Masgabriel.

At the South.
Habudiel, Uriel, Machasiel,
Naromiel, Charsiel.

Fumigation: Red Sandalwood.

Conjuration of the Lords day.

I conjure you and confirm over you; Angels of God, very strong and very holy, in the name of Adonay, Eye, Eye, Eye, who is He who was, is and will be, Eye, Abiaye, and in the name of Saday, Cados, Cados, Cados, who sits high above the Cherubim, and by the great name of this strong and powerful God, and who is exalted above all the Heavens, Eye, Saray, the Maker of the ages, who first created the world , the sky, the earth, the sea, and all things that are therein, and who has sealed them with his holy name Phaa, and by the names of the holy Angels who rule in the fourth army, and who serve in the presence of the most powerful Salamia, great and honored Angel; and by the name of the star which is the Sun, and by the sign and by the immense name of the living God, and by all the names mentioned above, I conjure you Michael, great Angel, who is appointed for Sunday, and by the name of Adonay, God of Israel, who created the world and all that is within, to work for me and to fulfill all my request according to my will and desire, in my work and my cause.

And here thou shalt declare thy cause and business, and for what thing thou makest this Conjuration.

The Spirits of the Air of the Lords day, are under the North-winde; their nature

SUNDAY.

Hours of the Day.	Angels of the Hours.
1. Yayn	Michael
2. Ianor	Anael
3. Nasnia	Raphael
4. Salla	Gabriel
5. Sadedali	Cassiel
6. Thamur	Sachiel
7. Ourer	Samael
8. Tanir	Michael
9. Néron	Anael
10. Jaye	Raphael
11. Abay	Gabriel
12. Natalon	Cassiel

Hours of the Night.	Angels of the Hours.
1. Beron	Sachiel
2. Barol	Samael
3. Thanu	Michael
4. Athir	Anael
5. Mathon	Raphael
6. Rana	Gabriel
7. Netos	Cassiel
8. Tafrac	Sachiel
9. Sassur	Samael
10. Aglo	Michael
11. Calerna	Anael
12. Salam	Raphael

is to procure Gold, Gemmes, Carbuncles, Riches; to cause one to obtain favour and benevolence; to dissolve the enmities of men; to raise men to honours; to carry or take away infirmities.

Common Forms of the Spirits of the Sun, on the Lords day.

They most often appear with a large and elongated body, bloody and coarse, of a golden color with a tincture of blood; their movement is the radiance and brilliance of the sky, and their sign is to excite sweat in him who conjures them and compels them to come to him.

Their particular forms are:
A king, a sceptre in hand, mounted on a lion; a king, crowned; a queen, holding a sceptre in hand; a bird; a lion; a rooster; a garment of saffron or gold color; a sceptre; a man with a tail.

Considerations of Monday.

The Angel of Monday, his Sigil, Planet, the Signe of the Planet, and name of the First Heaven:

Gabriel.

Shamain.

The Angels of Monday.
Gabriel, Michael, Samael.

The Angels of the Air ruling on Monday.
Arcan, King.

His Ministers: Bilet, Missabu, Abuzaha.

The winde under which are the Angels of the Air.
Zephyrus (The West-winde).

The Angels of the First Heaven, ruling on Monday, which ought to be called from the four parts of the World.

At the East.
Gabriel, Deamiel, Gabrael,
Janael, Madiel.

At the West.
Sachiel, Bachanael, Zaniel,
Corabiel, Habaiel.

At the North.
Mael, Baliel, Vuael,
Balay, Valnum, Humastrau.

At the South.
Curaniel, Hanun, Dabriel,
Anayl, Darquiel, Vetuel.

Fumigation of Monday : Aloes.

Conjuration of Monday.

I conjure you and confirm over you, strong and good Angels, in the name of Adonay, Adonay, Adonay, Eïè, Eïè, Eïè, Cados. Cados, Cados, Achim, Achim, Achim, Ja, Ja, of strong Ja, who appeared at Mount Sinai, with the glorification of king Adonay, Saday, Zebaoth, Amathoy, Ya, Ya, Ya, Marinata Abim, Jeia, who created on the second day the seas and the ponds and all the waters, both in the earth and on the earth. He has sealed the sea with his name Most High, and it will not pass the bounds that he has given it, and by the names of the Angels who rule in the first army, who serve Orphaniel, great, precious and honored Angel; and by the name of the star which is the Moon, and by the above mentioned names, I conjure you, Gabriel, who is in charge of Monday which is the second day, to work for me and accomplish, &c... (Here, like on Sunday, we specify what we want).

The Spirits of the Air of Monday, are subject to the West-winde, which is the winde of the Moon: their nature is to give silver; to convey things from place to place; to make horses swift, and to disclose the secrets of persons both present and future.

MONDAY.

Hours of the Day.	Angels of the Hours.
1. *Yayn*	*Gabriel*
2. *Ianor*	*Cassiel*
3. *Nasnia*	*Sachiel*
4. *Salla*	*Samael*
5. *Sadedali*	*Michael*
6. *Thamur*	*Anael*
7. *Ourer*	*Raphael*
8. *Tanir*	*Gabriel*
9. *Neron*	*Cassiel*
10. *Jayon*	*Sachiel*
11. *Abay*	*Samael*
12. *Natalon*	*Michael*

Hours of the Night.	Angels of the Hours.
1. *Beron*	*Anael*
2. *Barol*	*Raphael*
3. *Thanu*	*Gabriel*
4. *Athir*	*Cassiel*
5. *Mathon*	*Sachiel*
6. *Rana*	*Samael*
7. *Netos*	*Michael*
8. *Tafrac*	*Anael*
9. *Sassur*	*Raphael*
10. *Aglo*	*Gabriel*
11. *Calerna*	*Cassiel*
12. *Salam*	*Sachiel*

Common Forms of the Spirits of the Moon on Monday.

Their bodies are usually large, phlegmatic, their color like that of a dark and tenebrous cloud, their faces swollen, their eyes red and full of water, their heads bald, their teeth like wild boars. Their movements are similar to those of a great storm at sea. The sign which will manifest their approach to the Circle will be an abundant rain.

Their particular forms are:
Their particular forms are:
A king armed with a bow, with arrows, and mounted on a deer; a small child; a huntress armed with a bow and arrows; a cow; a little deer; a goose; a green or silver coloured outfit; an arrow; a multi-footed man.

Considerations of Tuesday.

The Angel of Tuesday, his sigil, his Planet, the Signe governing that Planet, and the name of the Fifth Heaven:

The Angels of Tuesday.
Samael, Satael, Amabiel.

The Angels of the Air ruling on Tuesday.
Samax, King.

His Ministers: Carmax, Ismoli, Paffran.

The winde under which are the Angels of the Air.
Subsolanus (The East-winde).

The Angels of the Fifth Heaven ruling on Tuesday, which ought to be called from the four parts of the World.

At the East.
Friagne, Galzas, Guael,
Arragon, Damael.

At the West.
Lama, Soncas, Irel,
Astagna, Iaxel, Lobquin, Isiael.

At the North.
Rahumel, Seraphiel, Hyniel,
Mathiel, Rayel, Fraciel.

At the South.
Sacriet, Osael, Ianiel,
Vianel, Galdel, Zaliel.

Fumigation of Tuesday: Pepper.

Conjuration of Tuesday.

I conjure and confirm over you, strong and holy Angels, by the name Ya, Ya, Ya, He, He, He, Va, Hy, Hy, Ha, Ha, Ha, Va, Va, Va, An, An, An, Aie, Aie, Aie, El, Ay, Elibra,

Eloim, Eloim: and by the names of this Most High God, who made the water dry and called it earth, who produced trees and herbs on its surface, and who sealed it with his holy, precious and adorable Name; and by the name of the Angels who rule in the fifth army, who serve Acimoy, great, strong, powerful and honored Angel; and by the name of the star which is Mars; and by the above mentioned names, I conjure you, Samael, great Angel who is in charge of Tuesday, and by the names of Adonay, living and true God, that you work for me and accomplish, &c... (as in the conjuration of Sunday).

The Spirits of the Air of Tuesday are under the East-winde: their nature is to cause wars, mortality, death and combustions; and to give ten thousand Soldiers at a time; to bring death, infirmities or health.

The manner of their appearing you may see in the former book.

TUESDAY.

Hours of the Day.	Angels of the Hours.
1. Yayn	Samael
2. Ianor	Michael
3. Nasnia	Anael
4. Salla	Raphael
5. Sadedali	Gabriel
6. Thamur	Cassiel
7. Ourer	Sachiel
8. Tanir	Samael
9. Neron	Michael
10. Jayon	Anael
11. Abay	Raphael
12. Natalon	Gabriel

Hours of the Night.	Angels of the Hours.
1. Beron	Cassiel
2. Barol	Sachiel
3. Thanu	Samael
4. Athir	Michael
5. Mathon	Anael
6. Rana	Raphael
7. Netos	Gabriel
8. Tafrac	Cassiel
9. Sassur	Sachiel
10. Aglo	Samael
11. Calerna	Michael
12. Salam	Anael

Common Forms of the Spirits of Mars on Tuesday.

They will appear for a long time with a bilious and very ugly face, of a slightly brown color, turning to red, having horns similar to those of a deer and the claws of a griffin. They bellow like raging bulls; their movement is like of a lit fire; and the sign that they are approaching the Circle is lightning and thunder.

Their particular forms are:
An armed king mounted on a wolf ; a red coat; an armed man; a woman holding a shield on her thigh; a goat; a horse; a deer; sheep's wool or fleece; a man with many heads.

Considerations of Wednesday.

The Angel of Wednesday, his Sigil, Planet, the Signe governing that Planet, and the name of the Second Heaven:

The Angels of Wednesday.
Raphael, Miel, Seraphiel.

The Angels of the Air, ruling on Wednesday.
Madiat, *or* Modiat, King.

His Ministers: Suquinos, Sallales.

The Angels of the Second Heaven govern Wednesday, which ought to be called from the four parts of the World.

At the East.
Mathlaï, Tarmiel, Baraborat.

At the West.
Jerescue, Mitraton.

At the North.
Thiel, Venahel, Veirnuel,
Rael, Vetel, Jariachel, Abuiori.

At the South.
Mittiel, Caluel, Netapa,
Vel, Babel, Laquel.

*The Wind under which are the Angels of the
Air governing on Wednesday.*
Africus (The Southwest-winde).

Fumigation of Wednesday: Mastic.

Conjuration of Wednesday.

*I conjure you and confirm over you, strong and
powerful Angels, in the name of the strong,
most formidable and blessed Ja, Adonay, Elohim,
Saday, Saday, Saday, Eye, Eye, Eye, As Amie,
Asaray; and in the name of Adonay, God of*

Israel, who created the great lights to distinguish day from night; and by the name of all the Angels who serve in the second army, in the presence of Tetra, the major Angel, strong and powerful, and by the name of the star which is Mercury, and by the name of the seal with which God, very strong and honored sealed it; by all the above mentioned things, I conjure you, Raphael, great Angel who is in charge of Wednesday which is the fourth day; and by the holy name which was written on the forehead of Aaron, the very high Priest of the Creator; and by the name of the Angels who are confirmed in the grace of the Savior; and by the name of the throne of the animals which have healthy wings, that you work for me, &c...

The Spirits of the Air of Wednesday are subject to the South-west-winde: their nature is to give all Metals; to reveal all earthly things past, present and to come; to pacific judges, to give victories in war, to re-edifie, and teach experiments and all decayed Sciences, and to change bodies mixt of Elements conditionally out of one into another; to give infirmities or

WEDNESDAY.

Hours of the Day.	Angels of the Hours.
1. *Yayn*	*Raphael*
2. *Ianor*	*Gabriel*
3. *Nasnia*	*Cassiel*
4. *Salla*	*Sachiel*
5. *Sadedali*	*Samael*
6. *Thamur*	*Michael*
7. *Ourer*	*Anael*
8. *Tanir*	*Raphael*
9. *Neron*	*Gabriel*
10. *Jayon*	*Cassiel*
11. *Abay*	*Sachiel*
12. *Natalon*	*Samael*

Hours of the Night.	Angels of the Hours.
1. *Beron*	*Michael*
2. *Barol*	*Anael*
3. *Thanu*	*Raphael*
4. *Athir*	*Gabriel*
5. *Mathon*	*Cassiel*
6. *Rana*	*Sachiel*
7. *Netos*	*Samael*
8. *Tafrac*	*Michael*
9. *Sassur*	*Anael*
10. *Aglo*	*Raphael*
11. *Calerna*	*Gabriel*
12. *Salam*	*Cassiel*

health; to raise the poor, and cast down the high ones; to binde or lose Spirits; to open locks or bolts: such-kinde of Spirits have the operation of others, but not in their perfect power, but in virtue or knowledge. The what manner they appear, it is before spoken.

Common Forms of the Spirits of Mercury on Wednesday.

They will most often appear with a body of average size, cold, damp, beautiful; of an affable conversation, of a human face like an armed man, of a brilliant and dazzling color; their movement is similar to that of a clear cloud; their sign is to cause great fear to the one who conjures them and makes them come to him.

Their particular forms are:
A king riding on a bear; a handsome young man; a woman holding a cattail; a dog; a bear; a magpie; a multi-coloured outfit; a rod; a stick.

Considerations of Thursday.

The Angel of Thursday, his Sigil, Planet, the Signe of the Planet, and the name of the Sixth Heaven:

The Angels of Thursday.
Sachiel, Castiel, Asasiel.

The Angels of the Air ruling on Thursday.
Guth, King.

His Ministers: Maguth, Gutriz.

The winde which the said Angels of the Air are under on Thursday.
Notus (The South-winde).

But because there are no Angels of the Air to be found above the Fifth Heaven, therefore on Thursday say the following prayers in the four parts of the World:

At the East.
O God, great and most high, and honored by all the infinite centuries.

At the West.
O wise, illustrious and fair God, and of divine clemency, I pray to you, my most pious Father, that I may today accomplish my request, my operation and my work, and make them perfectly: you who live and reign throughout all the infinite centuries of centuries. Amen.

At the North.
O God mighty, strong and without any beginning.

At the South.
O mighty and merciful God.

Fumigations of Thursday: Saffron.

Conjuration of Thursday.

I conjure and confirm over you, Holy Angels, by the name Cados, Cados, Cados, Eschercie, Eschercie, Eschercie, Hatim Ya, strong support of the centuries, Cantin, Jaym, Janic, Anie, Calbat, Sabbac, Berifay, Alnaym; and by the name Adonay, who on the fifth day created fish and reptiles in the waters, and birds on the earth flying to the Heavens; and by the names of the Angels who serve in the sixth army, in the presence of the Shepherd Angel, holy, great and powerful prince; and by the name of the star which is Jupiter; and by the name of his seal; and by the name of Adonay, sovereign God creator of all things; and by the name of all the stars, and by their strength and virtue, and by the names aforesaid, I conjure you, Sachiel, great Angel, who is appointed to Thursday, to work for me, and to accomplish, &c...

The Spirits of the Air of Thursday, are subject to the South-winde; their nature is to procure the love of woman; to cause men to be merry and joyful; to pacifie

THURSDAY.

Hours of the Day.	Angels of the Hours.
1. Yayn	Sachiel
2. Ianor	Samael
3. Nasnia	Michael
4. Salla	Anael
5. Sadedali	Raphael
6. Thamur	Gabriel
7. Ourer	Cassiel
8. Tanir	Sachiel
9. Neron	Samael
10. Jayon	Michael
11. Abay	Anael
12. Natalon	Raphael

Hours of the Night.	Angels of the Hours.
1. Beron	Gabriel
2. Barol	Cassiel
3. Thanu	Sachiel
4. Athir	Samael
5. Mathon	Michael
6. Rana	Anael
7. Netos	Raphael
8. Tafrac	Gabriel
9. Sassur	Cassiel
10. Aglo	Sachiel
11. Calerna	Samael
12. Salam	Michael

strife and contentions; to appease ene-mies; to heal the diseased, and to disease the whole; and procureth losses, or taketh them away.

Common Forms of the Spirits of Jupiter on Thursday.

They appear with a sanguine and bil-ious body, of average size, in a horrible and terrible movement; with a very gentle look, a pleasant conversation, of an iron color. Their movement is a flash accom-panied by the sound of thunder, and the sign that they will approach the Circle will be that it will seem to you as if being de-voured by lions.

Their particular forms are:
A king, with a drawn sword in hand, on a deer; a man dressed very long and wearing a mitre; a young girl adorned with flowers and crowned with laurel; a bull; a deer; a peacock; an azure-coloured outfit; a sword; a flute.

Considerations of Friday.

The Angel of Friday, his Sigil, his Planet, the Signe governing that Planet, and name of the Third Heaven:

The Angels of Friday.
Anael, Rachiel, Sachiel.

The Angels of the Air, ruling on Friday.
Sarabotes, King.

His Ministers.
Amabiel Aba, Abalidoth Flaef.

The Wind under which are the Angels of the Air.
Zephyrus (The West-winde).

Angels of the Third Heaven, ruling on Friday, which are to be called from the four parts of the World.

At the East.
Setchiel, Tamael, Chedusitaniel,
Tenaciel, Corat.

At the West.
Turiel, Kadie, Coniel,
Mattiel, Babiel, Kuffattiel.

At the North.
Peniel, Raphael, Penael,
Raniel, Penat, Doremiel.

At the South.
Porna, Samael, Sachiel,
Santanael, Chermiel, Faniel.

Fumigation of Friday: Pepperwort.

Conjuration of Friday.

I conjure and confirm you, strong, holy and powerful Angels, in the name of On, Hey, Heya, Ja, Ja, Adonay, Saday; and in the name of the same Saday who, on the sixth day, created the four-footed animals, the reptiles and men and gave Adam all power over the animals: therefore blessed be the name of the Creator in his place, and by the names of the Angels who serve in the third army in the presence of Dagiel, great Angel, strong and powerful prince; and by the name of the star which is Venus, and by its seal which is holy, and by the above mentioned names, I conjure you, Anael, who is in charge of Friday which is the sixth day, to work for me, &c...

The Spirits of the Air of Friday are subject to the West-winde; their nature is to give silver: to excite men, and incline them to luxury; to reconcile enemies through luxury; and to make marriages; to allure men to love women; to cause, or take away infirmities; and to do all things which have motion.

Common Forms of the Spirits of Venus on Friday.

They appear with a beautiful body, of medium size, with an amiable and pleas-

Friday.

Hours of the Day.	Angels of the Hours.
1. Yayn	Anael
2. Ianor	Raphael
3. Nasnia	Gabriel
4. Salla	Cassiel
5. Sadedali	Sachiel
6. Thamur	Samael
7. Ourer	Michael
8. Tanir	Anael
9. Neron	Raphael
10. Jayon	Gabriel
11. Abay	Cassiel
12. Natalon	Sachiel

Hours of the Night.	Angels of the Hours.
1. Beron	Samael
2. Barol	Michael
3. Thanu	Anael
4. Athir	Raphael
5. Mathon	Gabriel
6. Rana	Cassiel
7. Netos	Sachiel
8. Tafrac	Samael
9. Sassur	Michael
10. Aglo	Anael
11. Calerna	Raphael
12. Salam	Gabriel

ant appearance, of a white or green and sometimes golden color; their movement is similar to that of a very bright star; and for their signs, we will see near the Circle young girls frolicking and exciting the one who performs the operation to have fun with them.

Their particular forms are:
A king, a sceptre in hand, mounted on a camel; a perfectly well dressed young girl; a young girl completely naked; a goat; a camel; a dove; a white or green outfit; flowers; savin Juniper.

Considerations of Saturday.

The Angel of Saturday, his Seal, his Planet, and the Signe governing the Planet:

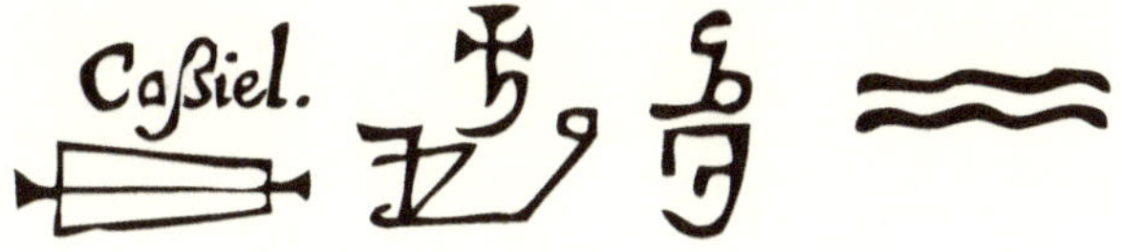

The Angels of Saturday.
Cassiel, Machalan, Uriel.

The Angels of the Air, ruling on Saturday.
Maymon, King.

His Ministers.
Abumalith, Assaibi, Balidet.

The Wind under which are the Angels of the Air.
Africus (The Southwest-winde).

Fumigation of Saturday: Sulphur.

It is already declared in the Consideration of Thursday, that there are no Angels ruling the Air, above the fifth heaven: therefore in the four Angles of the world, use those Orations which you see applied to that purpose on Thursday.

Conjuration of Saturday.

I conjure and confirm upon you, Caphriel or Cassiel, Iaehalori and Seraqueil, strong and powerful Angels, and by the name of Adonay, Adonay, Adonay, Eie, Eie, Eie, Acim, Acim, Acim, Cados, Cados, Cados, Inavel, Ima, Ima, Saday, Ia, Sar, the Lord who formed the centuries, and who rested on the seventh day; and by Him who of His good pleasure has given to the children of Israel as an inheritance this day to be kept exactly and sanctified, to then have its reward in the next age; and by the name of the Angels who serve in the seventh army, under the guidance and command of Booel, great Angel and powerful prince; and by the name of the star which is Saturn, and by its holy seal and by the above mentioned names; I conjure upon you, Caphriel, who is in charge of Saturday which is the seventh day, that you work for me, &c...

The Spirits of the Air of Saturday are subject to the Southwest-winde: the nature of them is to sow discordes, hatred, evil thoughts and cogitations; to give leave freely, to slay and kill every one, and to lame or maim every member.

Common Forms of the Spirits of Saturn on Saturday.

They most often appear long and slender, with a furious look, having four faces: one on the back, the other on the front of the head, these two faces having a beak; the other two faces are on their knees. They are black and transparent in color; their movement is a great agitation of winds, with an appearance of earthquakes. Their signal is to make the earth white, whiter than any snow.

SATURDAY.

Hours of the Day.	Angels of the Hours.
1. *Yayn*	*Cassiel*
2. *Ianor*	*Sachiel*
3. *Nasnia*	*Samael*
4. *Salla*	*Michael*
5. *Sadedali*	*Anael*
6. *Thamur*	*Raphael*
7. *Ourer*	*Gabriel*
8. *Tanir*	*Cassiel*
9. *Neron*	*Sachiel*
10. *Jayon*	*Samael*
11. *Abay*	*Michael*
12. *Natalon*	*Anael*

Hours of the Night.	Angels of the Hours.
1. *Beron*	*Raphael*
2. *Barol*	*Gabriel*
3. *Thanu*	*Cassiel*
4. *Athir*	*Sachiel*
5. *Mathon*	*Samael*
6. *Rana*	*Michael*
7. *Netos*	*Anael*
8. *Tafrac*	*Raphael*
9. *Sassur*	*Gabriel*
10. *Aglo*	*Cassiel*
11. *Calerna*	*Sachiel*
12. *Salam*	*Samael*

Their particular forms are:
A bearded king mounted on a dragon;
a bearded old man; an old woman leaning
on a stick; a pig; a dragon; an owl; a black
coat; a scythe; juniper.

OATHS & SUBMISSIONS
OF THE SPIRITS.

We dominant Spirits; namely, Kings, Emperors, Princes, Dukes, Counts, Marquis, Barons, Governor-Generals, Captains, Ministers, Lords & our other subjects the Spirits, acknowledge, under-sign, attest, bind & swear upon the high & most sacred names of God, the Conjurations & Exorcisms contained in this Book, as also the Characters belong-ing to us, to be of general value & ser-vice to all those who shall make use of the present Book in all their needs & neces-sities whatsoever, & without exemption, according to the power we have received from God, & we ratify all the following things.

FIRSTLY.

We pledge & submit ourselves to serve faithfully all those who shall hereby request us, according to our oath, & to do or cause to be done by our subjects all desires & wills, & that no mortal shall ever have knowledge of what shall be done & executed by our ministry, & that no Spirits shall be able to give knowledge of it to anyone, though they be invoked for it. We also promise to bring them or have them bring & transport whatever is required of us, without deceit or fraud, & that everything will be good & loyal to their will, without our being able to take it back either during their life or after their death, & that we cannot expect any reward for the services we render them.

Item. We submit ourselves to appear to all those who will call us by our names contained in this present Book, in beautiful human form, without any ugliness or deformity, whenever we are called, without doing any harm to what they have received from God, nor to their five senses of nature, nor to those who will be in their company, nor to the place or houses where they will call us & this without making noise, neither lightning, nor thunder, nor lightnings, nor clatter, nor rupture, nor fracture, nor uproar, in any way whatsoever, & no living creature will be aware of our coming, that those who will call us & their companions, if they order it to us; we also oblige ourselves to answer them on all questions & requests made to us, & our answers will be true without amphibology, nor double meaning; on the contrary, we will speak good English, precisely & intelligibly; & after having satisfied what is required of us, we will withdraw in peace & without tumult, observing the same conditions in going as in coming, when they pronounce the dismissal.

Item. For the execution of all the aforesaid conditions we oblige ourselves & commit ourselves, under the penalties of the hundredfold increase of our torments, from moment to moment, & of the deprivation of our offices, honours & dignities, in witness whereof we have affixed our seals, stamps & Characters, & signed the present Book, to serve all those who will invoke us, & immediately we will do what we are ordered without any delay.

Having discussed the nature of aerial Spirits, the Curious will have reason to be satisfied with them. If he wants something more extensive on this subject, he can have recourse to the Magic of Arbatel & the Steganography of Abbot Tritheme, the translation of which we will shortly give. It is now appropriate to speak of the infernal Spirits, and to give the calls to make them come, to command them and to make them to obey in all that we may require of them, by means of their characters contained in the black sheets which we will attach to this Work, as well as the Magical Ceremonies of Agrippa with a very curious collection of Secrets whose effects will be most surprising; & to diversify this present Treatise, we will also end it with the Secrets which follow.

OCCULT SECRETS

For Love.

On the first Friday of the Moon, buy a half-ell long red ribbon without haggling, in the name of the person you love; tie a knot, and do not tighten it, but say the *Pater noster* until *in tentationem*, and instead of saying *sed libera nos à malo*, you will say, *ludea, ludei, ludeo;* at the same time tighten the knot. On this day, say only one *Pater*, on the second, say two, and so on for nine days, tying a knot each day, tightening it only at *ludei*, &c. Then put this ribbon as it is on your left arm so that it touches the flesh. Touch the person for whom you have tied it, and she will do your will.

To make a Girl come.

Have three small black beans, place one between each finger of your right hand, put your hand like this on your flesh over the heart, then catch the person's gaze and pronounce the following: *Ego, ago, & superago, & consummatum est.*

Another on the same subject.

Take three beans or small white beans, and place them as above, placing your hand in the same way; then being looked at by the person, say: *Ebe, mebe, matristope.*

Against bladed Weapons.

Say while drawing the sword from its sheath: *Sancta Virgo immaculata,* Blessed Virgin Mary, preserve me from the bladed weapon, as you were preserved from original sin in your birth, as after your childbirth, by the Almighty. So be it.

Against Fire.

If you do not save me and help me, Lord, I agree to be confounded in Hell. Make three crosses on the mantelpiece with a coal taken from the fire.

Other.

Write with a fire coal, A. I. N. R. B. or *In te, Domine, speravi, non confundar in æternum.*

To have a familiar Spirit.

Have a very pure gold ring on a Thursday, in which you will have engraved the following: 35, 35, 35, after which go near a man who is about to die, and put it in his mouth. After his death, remove it; return three days later in your house, and say on your knees the *De profundis*, perfume the ring with rue, and conjure the Spirit by his baptismal name to answer you. First he will answer you;

command him to appear and enter the ring, and he will do so and remain with you always, to answer whatever you wish.

Those who wish to know more extensively about Necromancy or the art of bringing back souls from the past treasures in this world, will have recourse to the Grimoire of Pope Honorius.

To stop short one or several people.

Say: *Veide, Rougan, Rada, Bagabius,* put the right knee and wrist to the ground, roll over the body, and get up without the left touching anything.

To discover a Thief.

Make a galette; when it will be cooked, make as many pieces as you suspect there are people, on which you will write the following words: *Omax, Opax, Olifax.* Give them to eat, then, clasping your thumb in your hand, say subtly in a low voice in each person's ear: If you have stolen, flee in the name of the devil; if you have not stolen, flee in the name of God the Father, the Son and the Holy Spirit. Pronounce these words three times in a row, incontinently the one who is an accomplice will appear with his mouth full of foam, and will make restore the theft to you.

Against headaches.

Write on an Olive leaf : Athena. Bind this leaf to your head.

To prevent Dogs from barking.

Say as you enter their territory, and before they smell you: Terra, Farra, Garra, by the virtue of my left testicle, let us pass, I am off to debauchery. Repeat three times, holding your left testicle in your hand and turning it.

Mole Hand, guard for Horses.

On Ash Wednesday, one hour after noon, you will perform the following operation: being provided with a Mole and a small new knife, bought without haggling, you will go to the place where the Horses are, as in the stable, and make your little animal bleed at the neck, dropping a few drops of its blood on the head of your Horses one after the other, saying: May this blood that I sprinkle on my beast, serve to make it go and hasten in the name of the Father, and of the Holy Spirit. After which, skilfully skin the little animal, leaving the skin hanging from the four legs. Fill the skin, if you wish, with some hay to keep it stretched out, after which rub it three times in succession on the foreheads of your Horses, going from nose to ears, saying at the first time: *Ante*, at the second, *Ante te*, at the third, *super Ante te*, which you will do every morning as you enter the stable. You will observe to bury the little animal in the earth.

To shoe a Horse, however difficult it may be.

Say, circling the Horse: I conjure you in the name of God, and command you to let yourself be shod, to carry man, no more and no less than Jesus was carried in Egypt by the Virgin, *Pater, &c., Ave, &c.*

Guard for the Flock.

You will write above the two Pentacles shown here, traced and made on virgin parchment, the following words: Autheos ✠ Anastros ✠ Noxio ✠ Bay ✠ Gloy ✠ Aper ✠ Agia ✠ Agios ✠ Hischiros.

Deus Tetragrammaton misericors et pius, per ista sanctissima nomina et per ista sanctissima at tributa da mihi fortunam et horam bonam in omnibus meis factis, et libera me omni malo et perturbatione. Amen. Per Jesum Christum Filium tuum, Amen. Three *Credo,* &c.

This Pentacle must be made on parchment, as said; the Orisons above will be written on it, then a Mass will be said on it, and the Sheep will be rubbed with it, then it will be placed between two boards at the exit of the sheepfold, so that the flock may pass over it, then the said parchment will be removed and kept clean.

Orison of M. Saint Abraham, guard for Sheep.

Orison of God which was given to M. Saint Abraham, who was a shepherd for seven years in the forests of Ardennes, without a wolf or she-wolf having done any harm to him, nor to his body, nor to his lively flock of woolly beasts, here I am, and M. Saint Abraham, his lively flock leading on his path meets wolves and she-wolves (knee to the ground) in the name of the Father, and of the Son and of the Holy Spirit, and from M. Saint Laurent who closes and clenches his teeth, that of my lively flock of woolly beasts, you have no head to gnaw, nor any blood to suck, nor to misplace them, and by M. Saint Eustache, and by Mrs Saint Agatha, and by Mrs Saint Genevieve, and by M. Saint Abraham, and all his companions, from the stole, from the scarf of M. of Saint Hubert, be my flock, I ask of you, in the name of the Father, and of the Son and of the Holy Spirit. In the name of M. Saint Jean, through M. Saint Abraham, I also pray to God, the Virgin, all the good saints of Paradise, to keep for me this lively flock of woolly beats, healthy and clean, drinking well, eating well, fat and large, well boiled, well bodied, well swollen, closed and enclosed around me, as I believe, in the name of the Father and the Blessed Virgin, and of all the good Saints of Paradise.

Further instructions for guards, both of Horses and Sheep, can be found in the Grimoire of Pope Honorius, and well as in the Clavicles of Solomon.

To draw the white ticket at the Militia.

Write the following on virgin parchment: It is also that the ticket that
is drawn is white, as it is true that God
appeared on the mountain to Moses and
Elysium, and that the law was truly pro-
tested by Gamaliel. You must carry it on
the arm from which you are drawing, and
pronounce the words while doing so.

Another against the Militia.

Make the following Pentacle on virgin parchment at the day and hour
of Jupiter or Venus, who are the enemies
of Mars, and perfume it with incense,
olive oil and a spider. You will carry this
Pentacle on the right arm, and while you
draw lots, pronounce the words written in
the circle, beginning with *Domine, fiat, &c.*

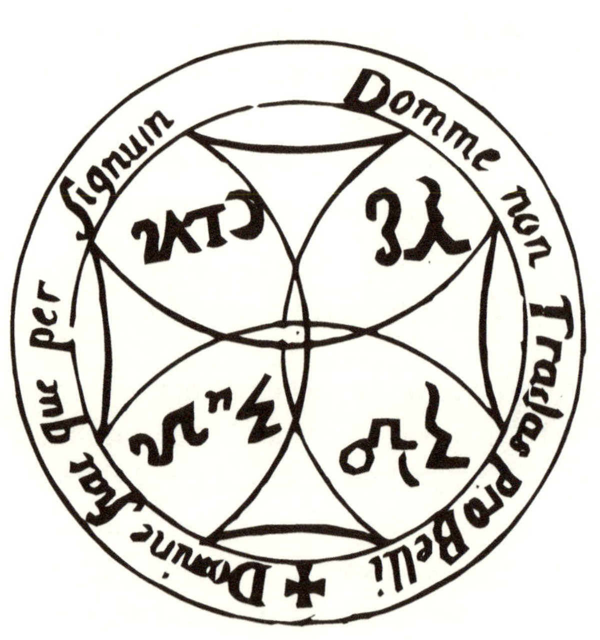
Domine non Tradas per Bellii
+ Domine fac que per signum

Orison of Pope Leo to lift all spells & enchantments.

Lasgaroth, ✠ Aphonidos, ✠ Palatia, ✠ Urat, ✠ Condion, ✠ Lamacron, ✠ Foudon, ✠ Arpagon, ✠ Alamar, ✠ Bourganis veniat Serebani.

This Orison, although brief, is nevertheless of great virtue. Others can be found in the Enchiridion, of which we will soon give a translation, with an ample Clavicle. We can still have recourse to the scourge of Demons, the whip of Demons, the flight of Demons, the dispersion of Demons, remedies against curses and the manual of Exorcisms all recently translated, for the cure of all magical illnesses.

To avoid the pain of torture.

Swallow a slip of paper with the following written in your blood: ✠ Aglas ✠ Aglanas ✠ Algadena ✠ imperubi es meritis ✠ tria pendent corpora ramis dismeus et gestus in medio et divina potestas dimeas clamator, sed jestas ad astra levatur; or again: ✠ Tel ✠ Bel ✠ Quel ✠ Caro ✠ Mon ✠ Aqua ✠.

For a sure shot.

Write on a small piece of paper: *Gaspard, Balthazard, Melchior, lead my pellet to the animal I want to shoot.* Stuff it with this slip, and recite the same words as you fire.

Against ringworm.

Saint Peter on the bridge of God sat, Our Lady of Caly came to him and said: *Peter, what are you doing here? Lady, it is for the evil of my chief that I m here. Saint Peter, you will rise in Saint Aget, you will go, you will take some holy ointment from the mortal wounds of Our Lord, you will grease yourself with it, and three times you will say, Jesus, Maria.* You must make three signs of the cross on your head.

Enchantment for blood.

In the blood of Adam came death; in the blood of Christ came life. O blood, stop!

To make a Rooster immortal.

Write the following on a piece of paper: *Ante, Ante te, super Ante te.* Make a Rooster swallow it, and recite the same words three times in its beak; then nail its head to the table with a new nail; remove the nail, it will not die.

To avoid being robbed.

Wear the following verses:
Imparibus mertis tria corpora ramis:
Dismas & gesmas medio divina potestas,
Alta petit infelix infirma gesmas:
Nos & res nostras conservet summa potestas:
Hos versus dicas, nec tu furto tua perdas.

Divination.

Make a cross in a crystal with olive oil, and under the cross write: *Saint Helen.* Then give a virgin child, born of legitimate marriage, a vial to hold, then kneel behind him, and say the following orison three times: *Deprecor, Domina S. Helena, mater regis Constantini, &c.* And when the child sees the Angel, he will be able to make the desired request.

To prevent Sheep from taking gobs.

Write the following verse on a piece of paper: *Super aspidem & basilicum ambulabis leonem & draconem.* Bring the Sheep out of the sheepfold or park, and rub them with this paper, uttering the same words.

To have recent memory of what happened a long time ago.

S ay the following for nine days, during the sacrifice of the Mass: *Collocavit it-erinus sumptu aglu redde perris diabolus infer-norum negromantium Salo* ✠ *Pato* ✠ *Belbuch* ✠ *Iterbuch* ✠ *Salio* ✠ *Azinum.* Make as many signs of the cross as they are marked between the words above.

Against Hæmorrhoids.

W ith the middle finger of your right hand, take saliva from your mouth and touch the hæmorrhoids while saying: *Pins, go away, God curses you in the name of the Father, the Son and the Holy Spirit.* Then say nine *Pater* and nine *Ave.* This is done for nine days; the second day only say eight, and each day is reduced in reverse order.

Against a firearm.

Write the following on a piece of paper and swallow it: *Armisi sarisi restingo*. When in danger, recite the same words.

For Love.

Buy four ells of fire-coloured ribbon, without haggling and without affecting anything, then go to Mass. Place yourself facing the person you wish to be loved, so that you can see him or her face to face, then say at the moment of the elevation, holding your ribbon in your hand, which will be bent into a cross like the rosette of a rosary: *Creature that I see with my eyes, it is as true that your heart will be bound to mine, as it is true that my sweet Saviour Jesus Christ was bound to the tree of the Cross, and as true that he is bound to the sacramental species that the Priest holds in his hands.*

Against all kinds of Fevers.

When Jesus saw the Cross on which his body was placed, his body trembled and his blood ran cold. A Jew named Marquantin came up to him and said: *I think you are afraid, or that the fevers have got you. No, replied Jesus, I am not afraid, nor do fevers hold me.* But whoever says this orison, to his right arm shall wear it, neither fever nor chill shall ever have. *Tertian fever, half-tertian fever, quartan fever, half-quartan fever, slow fever, daily fever, intermittent fever, malignant fever, purple fever, fever of whatever kind you may be, fever of whatever nature you may be, I conjure you to leave the body of N... in the name of the Father* ✠ *and of the Son* ✠ *and of the Holy Spirit* ✠ *and of M. saint Peter and Mrs his Mother;* who will cure him of the fever, if he is a man, or who will cure her, if she is a woman.

This paper is folded, saying *in the name of the Father, &c.,* then it is attached to the right arm of the Feverish, with five needle-length of crimson thread, saying also *in the name of the Father, &c.* It must be worn for nine days. It must be put on while on an empty stomach.

Against the Gout.

Say for nine days on an empty stomach: *Terra pestem tenero salene, salene, salene, salene manere his hire pedibus.* Then kiss the earth and spit on it.

Against Fevers.

Carry a paper for nine days, with the following written on it: *Abren d'Abrea.* Put it on at the first sign of fever, and during this time say, while fasting, five *Pater* and five *Ave* in honour of the five wounds of Jesus Christ.

Against Hemorrhagia.

Make a small cross of grass or wood, place it behind the neck, then say: *Angelus Domini annuntiat Mariæ & concepit de Spiritu sancto, Ave, Maria, &c., Ancilla Domini, fiat mihi secundum verbum tuum, Ave, Maria, &c. Et verbum caro factum est & habitavit in nobis, Ave, Maria, &c.*

Garter for walking & to guard against all perils & dangers.

Take some scarlet, make it into a garter that can encircle your hock; and on it, put nine hairs from a hanged man, then buy some white satin the length of the scarlet, on which you will write with your blood the following: *Verbum caro factum est, & habitabit in nobis.* Put the said satin on the scarlet, and let the words touch the hair. Tie this garter on your left hock, the satin against the flesh; as soon as you have arrived, remove the garter to use it again when necessary; have your bed bathed in sugar, and wash the soles of your feet with wine.

To cure a blocked Horse.

We take it with the right hand on the right side, saying: *Ego ago, & superago, & consummatum est,* then we make it move back two or three steps.

To know & conciliate one's Genie.

The pious and the wise will preserve those to whom they teach the orison in the following form, by which one invokes the help of God, sovereign Captain of Angels, in order to acquire the knowledge and friendship of one's genie.

God almighty and eternal, who formed all creatures for your honour and glory, and for the service of man, I beseech you to send me my good Angel N... who is (here we must name the Planet which governs him) to instruct me and inform me of the things about which, with justice and piety, I shall question him, and so that he may lead me in the things which are necessary for me to know in the arts and experiments of our ancient Fathers and Philosophers, or to obtain the way to preserve health, and to sustain life, and the means to be delivered from my enemies; but may your will be done and not mine, through Jesus Christ Our Lord. So be it.

The sages used to search first for the name and nature of the good Angel or genie of the one born, then they would endeavour to make him familiar and affable by convocations, adoration, prayers, characters, or other such ceremonies.

When we want to find him, let us above all look for the hour of birth, the Lord of the eleventh house; let us find what Olympic Spirit is attributed to this Planet, and besides that what Angel is given to the sign, in which the Lord was found. After examining how these two Spirits fit with each other, we must also consider the Spirit of the Lord of the eleventh house, so that the Spirits of the Planet relate more with them or do not fit; thus the state of the child's life will be at most constant or inconstant.

Some rightly take the Spirit of the Lord of the first house to be the Genie of birth, until we know more about this birth. We must not only consider the Spirit of this house and of the Moon in which this generation takes place, but we must also take care which wind of the region or of the angle of the world blows more strongly, which element predominates much more than the others in this time where the point of birth is located: that is, whether the weather is frosty, windy or rainy, or exposed to the rigours of cold. For by this observation we shall know the predominant element, and by means of it, the most powerful Spirit, and among the elements we shall choose the one that predominates.

Once this has been observed, it will not be impossible to draw advantages or obstacles from the Genie of birth, so that we will know which planet is the Domain, which house the Lord and assistance, which wind blows, which element is the empire, and which place, that is which region or city, can give more or less to the Genie of the child. Now, in this way, undoubtedly done with zeal, we can discover these things by observing and contemplating them with serious attention.

Divination by the Angel Uriel.

Put a white tablecloth on a table, place two new candles on it, take a very clean crystal glass, fill it with fountain water, put this glass on the table with a penny marked with a cross under the stem, sprinkle it with holy water, saying:

Benedictio Dei Patris omnipentis descendat super vos & maneat semper. In nomine Patris, & Filii & Spiritus Sancti. Amen.

Then kneel, bareheaded before the table, and say the following:

Holy Angels, Angels Holy, White Angel, my good Angel, I beseech you to deliver anything that may prevent Uriel from showing me what I wish to see, and to know in all truth, as it is true that God has destined you for my keeping: and for your reward, I will say the Pater *with the* Credo *and the* Miserere.

Then you will say thrice the following conjuration:

Saint Uriel, I conjure you by the great living God, who is your Master and mine, by the virginity of St John the Baptist and by the virginity that presents itself to you through the rod of Moses, that you come into this glass full of water; and that you do not leave until you have answered me to everything I will ask of you, Galate, Galata, Calin, Cala. Be welcome, bring the book of Moses, open it, place your hand on it, and swear to let me see what I wish to see, I shall say a Pater *to Jesus Christ, and an* Ave *to the Virgin Mary.*

When you see something in the glass, you will say:

Saint Uriel, I conjure you by the living God to make me see what I shall name to you: I promise you a Pater *and an* Ave.

Dismissal.

Ite in pace ad loca vestra, sit pax inter nos & vos. In nomine Patris, &c.

Reflection on the above operation & the difference observed in it.

It is not believed to be absolutely neces-sary to use the two candles, and to say that we can also operate with respect to ourselves. When one has done it without promising anything at all to this Angel, one has not always succeeded. When you look at this presentation, it is clear that something has been omitted, because you have to start with *in principio*, then the Litany and the seven Psalms.

This operation requires a virgin child, who, as soon as he sees the Angel in the glass, instruct him the requests and questions about which revelation is desired.

Other curious divinations can be found in the Clavicles of Solomon.

ORISON
To cure all kinds of illnesses.

Per Christum & cum Christo, & in Christo tibi Deo, Patri omnipotenti, & unitate

Spiritus sancti omnis honor & gloria. Per omnia secula seculorum. Oremus. Præceptis salutaribus moniti, & divinâ institutione formati, audemus dicere, Pater noster qui es cælis, &c. Amen. Jesus pentia patris, sapienta filii, virtus Spiritus sancti, sanet hoc vulnus ab omni malo Amen.

Jesus Domine, Jesus Christe, credo quod nocte Jovis in cœna postquam lavasti pedes tuorum, accepisti panem sanctissimis minibus tuis, & benedixisti & fregisti, & dedisti tuis Apostolis, dicens, accipite & comedite, hec est enim corpus meum, cimiliter accepisti calicem in sanctissimos manus & gratias egisti & tradidisti illis, dicens, accipite & bibite, quia hic est meus sanguis novi testamenti, qui pro multis effundetur in remissionem peccatorum, hæc quotiescum que feceritis, facite in meam commemorationem.

Obsecro te, mi Domine Jesus Christe, ut per hæc, sanctissima verba, & per virtutem illorum, & per meritum sanctissimæ passionis tuæ sanetur hoc vulnus, & malum issu. Amen. Jesus. In nomine Pains & Filii, & Spiritus sancti. Amen.

Table.

OCCULT SECRETS

End of Table.